SIZZLING Celebrities

Drake!

HIP-HOP CELEBRITY

BY ALLY AZZARELLI

Enslow Publishers, Inc.
40 Industrial Road
Box 398
Berkeley Heights, NJ 07922
USA

http://www.enslow.com

To Amanda Johnson, a Drake fan

Library of Congress Cataloging-in-Publication Data:

Azzarelli, Ally.

   Drake! : hip-hop celebrity / Ally Azzarelli.
      p. cm. — (Sizzling celebrities)
   Includes index.
   Summary: "Read about Drake's early life, how he got started in music, and his future plans"—Provided by publisher.
   ISBN 978-0-7660-4168-4
   1. Drake, 1986—Juvenile literature. 2. Rap musicians—United States—Juvenile literature. I. Title.
   ML3930.D73A99 2014
   782.421649092—dc23
   [B]   2012040312

Future editions:
Paperback ISBN: 978-1-4644-0275-3
EPUB ISBN: 978-1-4645-1174-5
Single-User PDF ISBN: 978-1-4646-1174-2
Multi-User PDF ISBN: 978-0-7660-5803-3

Printed in China

012013 Leo Paper Group, Heshan City, Guangdong, China

10 9 8 7 6 5 4 3 2 1

Photo Credits: AP Photo/Arthur Mola, pp. 23, 33, 38, 41; AP Photo/Brian Kersey, p. 36; AP Photo/Chris Pizzello, pp. 14, 24; AP Photo/Darren Calabrese, p. 29; AP Photo/John Minchillo, p. 30; AP Photo/L.M. Otero,p. 8; AP Photo/Matt Sayles, pp. 4, 18, 26, 43; AP Photo/Mike Brown, p. 7; AP Photos/Rich Pedroncelli, p. 45; AP Photo/Tammy Arroyo, p. 11; AP Photo/Wilfredo Lee, p. 15; Enslow Publishers, Inc., p. 15; John Steel/Shutterstock.com, p. 1.

Cover Photo: AP Photo/Chris Pizzello.

Contents

Meet Drake

Drake's start in showbiz came in an unlikely place. A classroom! "There was a kid in my class. [His] father was an agent. His dad would say, 'If there's anyone in the class that makes you laugh, have them audition for me.' After the audition he became my agent." At fifteen, Drake got a role on the teen drama, *Degrassi: The Next Generation*. Life was about to change.

Grammy-nominated Aubrey "Drake" Graham isn't the typical rapper. He's Canadian. He's biracial. And he's Jewish. "I don't want to limit my music to people based on their race and/or age," Drake admitted to *Hip Hop Canada* reporters. "I want everybody to be able to enjoy it. Being biracial and young, along with being American and Canadian [allows me to] try and cover all the bases ... I think with the right person and the right music, people from all walks of life can come together. I know that's what my life was about. I've seen it all, so that's what I want to bring to the table."

A Star Is Born
Aubrey "Drake" Graham was born on October 24, 1986, in Toronto, Ontario, Canada. Drake's father, Dennis Graham

◄ *Drake gestures during a performance at the Black Entertainment Television (BET) Awards on June 27, 2010, in Los Angeles.*

was a drummer. His mom, Sandi, was a teacher. Drake's mom is Jewish, and his father is African American. Drake's dad lived in Memphis, Tennessee, before he moved to Canada.

At just three, Drake would make up his own words to songs. He was also outgoing and loved to act and sing. When he was five, his mom got him an agent. She knew he had talent. As a youngster, he trained with Young People's Theatre and the Showtime summer workshop. He began modeling. Soon he landed commercials for Sears, GMC, and Toys 'R' Us.

Drake's folks split up when he was five years old. This divorce wasn't easy for the rapper. "I had to become a man very quickly and be the backbone for a woman who I love with all my heart, my mother," he said in an ABC interview.

Like many children of divorce, Drake lived with his mom. Since he was an only child, his mother didn't want him to get lonely. She kept him busy. He was involved in many activities. Drake's mom signed him up for hockey and summer camp. She felt that sports would help make him a team player.

Drake studied at a Jewish day school. He practiced these teachings throughout his youth. Jewish boys turning thirteen, have a Bar Mitzvah. "I had a Bar Mitzvah in an Italian restaurant," Drake told a reporter for a Jewish publication. For Drake, having a Bar Mitzvah meant he was now responsible for his actions. This was a very special day in his life—a Jewish boy becomes a man at age thirteen.

Talent Runs in the Family

Growing up, Drake would spend summers visiting his dad in Memphis. "I use to hold him in my lap," Drake's dad told TV reporters. "I use to hold him in my office while I played the piano, so this is how it got started." He went on to say, "That's why his metaphors are so phenomenal now because he's been in Memphis."

▲ *Sun Studio is just one of the musical places in Memphis, Tennessee.*

Drake comes from a long line of musicians. His dad, Dennis, played drums for Jerry Lee Lewis, a famous rock and roll musician. Drake's uncles, Larry Graham and Teenie Hodges, are also musicians. Drake's uncle Larry was a bass player. Larry played in the funk band Sly and the Family Stone. Uncle Teenie played lead guitar for Al Green. Al Green was a popular singer in the 1970s.

▲ *Al Green was one of the musicians that Drake admired when he was growing up.*

Life in the music biz isn't always easy. Musicians spend a lot of time on the road. Sadly, Drake's dad wasn't always there for him. "He chose to not be a dad at times. That's something I'll never be able to respect that much," Drake told TheHipHopUpdate.

However, Drake credits his dad for giving him his gift of music. "My dad is a great writer. [He is] naturally talented and naturally charming. He embodies that back-in-the-day cool." In Drake's song, "The Winner," Drake gives his mom, uncle, and grandma sweet shout-outs. He then adds, "And to my dad even though we was apart. I couldn't leave you out, you forever in my heart."

Not-so-Cool in School

Looking back at his early acting career, Drake can laugh. "I grew up through the awkward phases on television. The worst haircuts and the worst outfits are documented," Drake told radio station B96 about his days growing up on *Degrassi*.

Today Drake is a hip, famous rapper. However, he didn't always fit in. "I always felt like an outsider," Drake told reporter Katie Couric. "I went to an all Jewish school and being biracial and being Jewish, I was kind of connected to the kids, but like sort of distant. When kids are young, they don't understand everything. It can get a little cruel and a little mean. I got [teased]."

It is hard to picture someone as cool as Drake being teased. "Kids in class made fun of me all the time. I was never popular." confessed Drake to RedAlertLive.com. Success is sweet revenge on those bullies. Today Drake is selling out concerts. He has tens of thousands of adoring fans. "I wasn't cool. I'm cool now though. Things change. I really just want to be something positive for this generation," the singer added.

Breaking into Stardom

Most rappers don't start off as TV stars. Drake's career is sometimes compared to Will Smith's. Smith had some hit songs and starred on the 1990's show *The Fresh Prince of Bel-Air*. Though flattered, Drake told ABC, "I just want to be Drake. I just want to be me."

From 2001 to 2009, Drake played Jimmy Brooks on *Degrassi: The Next Generation*. The Canadian drama filmed at schools near his home. This helped him get an audition and land the part. The show is about the ups and downs of being a teen. In a way, Drake is as unique as his TV character, Jimmy.

Jimmy was a high school basketball star. Sadly Jimmy's life took a shocking turn. A classmate shot Jimmy near his locker. The scene was very real and very scary. This event changed the basketball player's life. From then on, Jimmy could no longer use his legs. He had to find new skills. This role helped Drake score five Young Artist Award nominations. In 2002, he and the *Degrassi* cast were proud winners. They won the Best Ensemble in a TV Series (Comedy or Drama) that year.

His dad said his son was shy about singing on records at first. However, Dennis encouraged him, "Drake, you've got a beautiful voice," Dennis told his son. Today his dad is proud of his famous rapper son. "My God, I look at him and I think, 'Oh, my God, this kid's got it.' I said, 'Drake, you've done it man.'"

Fitting in

Going to an all-white school wasn't easy for Drake. He was surrounded by wealthy kids. His classmates wore designer clothes. They drove fancy cars. To fit in, Drake would borrow his uncle's drop-top Lexus. Sometimes he'd rent expensive cars.

"Going to Forest Hill was definitely an interesting way of growing up," the rapper confessed to InterfaithFamily.com. "When you're young and unaware that the world is made up of different people, it is tough growing up. But me being different from everyone else just made me a lot stronger."

▼ *Drake poses with his Degrassi: The Next Generation costars (from left: Shane Kippel, Drake, Stacey Farber, and Adamo Ruggiero) at the 2007 Teen Choice Awards.*

Drake Quits High School

Many rappers are raised on tough city streets. Drake wasn't. He lived in a wealthy Toronto town. Drake studied at Forest Hill Collegiate Institute. However, Drake quit high school to pursue a music career.

"High School just wasn't for me," Drake told MTV's *When I Was 17*. "I was in History class and the teacher and I used to just go at it. Something just clicked. I just got up. Put my stuff in my bag … and [the teacher] said, 'If you do that, don't come back.'"

This was one of the hardest things Drake had to admit to his mom. "I brought so little trouble into my mother's household. When I did do something drastic, it was always for a good reason," the singer said. "She was upset, because I was close to finishing." Looking back, Drake is not proud of quitting school.

Drake's mom trusted him. Though not thrilled, she knew his heart was in his music. "She's been the most supportive person I've ever had in my life," Drake said in an MTV interview. "She's the only person that loves me unconditionally, really, I think."

Working Toward His Dream

Degrassi gave Drake a chance to show off his vocal skills. A few episodes featured Jimmy rapping. While still working on *Degrassi*, Drake began releasing mix tapes. A mix tape is a common industry term for an independently released MP3 download, CD, or streamed music. In Drake's case, he made his first release, *Room for Improvement*, available to his Web site and Myspace fans, in February 2006. This album was only available online. He sold about six thousand copies. Drake had no idea how his life was about to change.

After a taste of success with his 2006 mix tape, Drake released a second tape in 2007 called *Comeback Season*. It rocked! It featured his hit song "Replacement Girl." Drake nailed it with this tune. He even caught the attention of BET. "Replacement Girl" was honored on BET's *106 & Park*. On April 30, 2007, he had a huge accomplishment—he became the first unsigned Canadian rapper to have his music video featured on BET.

At this point, the future of Drake's acting career was uncertain. There were some changes to the *Degrassi* storylines. He was about to lose his part on the show. This is common for actors.

▲ *Drake joins Lil Wayne for a performance at the BET Awards on June 28, 2009.*

They know a TV role can't last forever. Drake loves music and wanted to make money doing what he loves best. Drake needed his luck to turn around—and fast. If not, he might have to find a "regular" job. He didn't want to abandon his goals.

Thanks to MySpace, Drake's music was passed on to rap star Lil Wayne. "We were introduced through a gentleman from Houston named Jazz Prince," Drake told Katie Couric. "He found me on MySpace and loved my music. He was like, 'Man, I know Lil Wayne and I'm gonna play him your music one day.' And I was like 'Yeah right.' I didn't [believe] it at first."

Things were about to change for the singer. In 2008, Drake got a surprising call from Lil Wayne. The famous rapper had a special request. He asked Drake to hop on a plane to Houston, Texas. Lil Wayne wanted him to join his tour. Not tomorrow or next week, but TONIGHT!

▼ *Drake (right) and Lil Wayne not only perform together, but also are friends. Here they are taking in an NBA finals game between the Miami Heat and the Chicago Bulls.*

While on tour, Drake and Lil Wayne recorded a couple songs together, including "I Want this Forever," "Ransom," and the remix to Drake's song "Brand New."

During this time, Drake was honored for a few different awards in the music industry. The Teen Choice Awards are voted on by young adults aged 13-19. They vote on the year's biggest achievements in music, movies, sports, and television. Drake has been nominated for nine awards, winning with the *Degrassi* cast in 2005 and 2007.

The Young Artist Award honors the best in African-American music and entertainment. Drake won one award for his role in *Degrassi*.

Rise to Stardom

The tour with Lil Wayne was huge for Drake. Because of its success, and the fact that Drake's time at *Degrassi* had ended, there was no turning back. In February 2009, Drake released his third mix tape, *So Far Gone.* This mix tape truly launched Drake's music career. Record label executives made him offers, but Drake kept putting off signing a record deal. Rumors circulated about who Drake would sign with. But in the summer of 2009, Drake finally got exactly what he wanted.

Drake signed a $2 million record deal with Lil Wayne's Young Money Entertainment. *So Far Gone* was rereleased in September 2009. This version was an extended play (EP) album, which is shorter than a normal album. The EP included five songs from the original mix tape along with two new songs.

The *So Far Gone* EP had guest appearances by Lil Wayne, Trey Songz, Bun B, and Young Jeezy. Three fan favorite singles from this EP are "Best I Ever Had," "Successful," and "I'm Goin' In." "Successful" and "Best I Ever Had" reached the No. 2 spot on *Billboard*'s Hot 100.

▲ *Drake and Young Jeezy perform at the BET Awards on June 27, 2010.*

From coast to coast, fans spent big bucks to see Drake. He sold out shows in minutes! In 2009, fans paid $80 a pop to see him at a small club in Washington, D.C.

That year, Drake was part of the *America's Most Wanted* tour with Lil Wayne, Young Jeezy, and Soulja Boy. However, Drake suffered a nasty fall onstage during a performance in Camden,

New Jersey. "I didn't really get any approval from my doctor," Drake told MTV. "But I made a personal decision 48 hours ago that I'd be letting a lot of people down if I didn't show up and at least show them I'm there for them." He tore his ACL, an important knee ligament that helps keep the body steady and stable. The singer had to have surgery. He was told if he had one more tear, he might not walk again.

Making Music

Drake's lyrics set him apart from other rappers. Critics give him a hard time about being sensitive. However, his fans love that about him. Drake respects the classic singers from the 60s and 70s like Curtis Mayfield, Marvin Gaye, and Al Green. "I don't understand our generation where nobody is allowed to really express any real emotion," Drake told the *LA Times*. "I think that's a scary place to be for our youth. I know there's always going to be close-minded people. But I think I make it so accessible. It's not tear your shirt off in the rain R&B. It's got a purpose."

In April 2010, *So Far Gone* won Rap Recording of the Year at the 2010 Juno Awards. The Juno Awards are special awards given to Canadian musicians. *So Far Gone* went "gold" on July 4, 2010, for selling more than 500,000 records.

Drake's 2010 *Light Dreams & Nightmares* tour was a big success. Two shows at Radio City Music Hall sold out in less than one hour. Performances in Miami and Atlanta were also sold out. In fact, *Billboard* reported 80 percent of all his concerts sold out before the tour even began.

Drake talked to Canada's *Much Music* about his fans. "People get funny around me," Drake said. "Like, 'Oh man, my heart's beating faster.' My heart beats faster too. My knees get weak too. I can't believe there are kids that waited out there for 20 hours. People slept in the rain, voices gone, sick ... all just for a ten second interaction. That's why I stayed there for six hours today ... It's not in my heart to be like, 'Next! Gimme your CD. Let's go!' That's not me."

In November 2009, Lil Wayne announced that Drake's very first album, *Thank Me Later*, was complete. The album was released on June 15, 2010. *Thank Me Later* features these four chart-topping hit singles: "Find Your Love," "Over," "Miss Me" with Lil Wayne, and "Fancy" with rappers T.I. and Swizz Beatz.

The same day that the album was released, Drake did a New York City Best Buy record signing. Fans camped out overnight just to get a glimpse of the rapper. They lined up in homemade Drake T-shirts and held signs. A Best Buy manager told MTV they needed twice as many security guards than normal to handle the fans.

To celebrate *Thank Me Later*'s release, Drake also planned to perform a free show at New York City's South Street Seaport. This drew a massive crowd! More than 25,000 fans lined up at the seaport. The city wasn't prepared for so many people. A riot almost broke out. Police were forced to cancel the show. Drake felt really bad about that. "I am so disappointed," Drake tweeted. "To all the devoted fans that came out, I wish you could have seen what I had planned."

Thank Me Later featured collaborations with Alicia Keys, The Dream, Jay-Z, Kanye, and Lil Wayne. It was a huge hit for Drake. The album debuted at number one on both American and Canadian charts. More than 447,000 copies were sold in the first week. *Thank Me Later* went platinum in just five weeks! This means that it sold more than one million copies.

In April 2011, a Pennsylvania Web site ran an article about the Stroudsburg Sherman Theater. For the first time in history, the theater sold out in minutes. Drake added a second show. The venue had never sold that many tickets so fast. People bought $350 scalped tickets to his UC Davis Pavilion show in California.

Take Care Leaks

His album *Take Care* was set to drop on November 15, 2011. One week earlier, fans heard it online. The leaked version wasn't as long as the official *Take Care* album. But it was enough to get fans pumped to buy the real deal.

"I am not sure if the album leaked," Drake tweeted when he first heard about the leak. "But if it did, thank God it doesn't happen a month early anymore." A few minutes later he tweeted fans, "Listen enjoy it, buy it if you like it ... and take care until next time."

Drake spoke to *Billboard* about the leaks saying, "I think that giving people the opportunity to judge before they go and buy, I think that can only help." He added, "There's a loyal fan base that's gonna go and support you just based off the fact that they want to own a copy of your material, and they know what it means to give you that one sale, and they hope that there's another hundred, two hundred, three hundred … people that are gonna do the same thing."

Drake Takes Care

Drake's second album, *Take Care*, was released as scheduled in mid-November 2011. It debuted at number one on the U.S. *Billboard* 200 chart. A whopping 631,000 copies were sold in the very first week. The album is certified platinum. More than 1,583,000 copies were sold in America alone!

This album produced four hit singles. They include the title track, "Take Care" with Rihanna, "Make Me Proud" with Drake's close friend Nicki Minaj, "The Motto" with rapper Lil Wayne, and "Headlines." *Take Care* hit number one in both the United States and Canada.

Critics and fans were very happy with *Take Care*. Drake explained to BBC Radio, "I didn't get to take the time that I wanted to on [*Thank Me Later*]. I rushed a lot of the songs and sonically I didn't get to sit with the record and say, 'I should change this verse.' Once it was done, it was done. That's why my new album is called *Take Care* because I got to take my time this go-round."

Drake was truly blown away by his Toronto *Take Care* CD signing in November 2011. He thought he was going to sign a few albums. Hundreds of fans showed up! Fans came from as far away as Bermuda and far-off towns in Canada just for a quick meeting with the rapper.

▲ *Drake poses with a poster advertising his album* Take Care *on November 14, 2011.*

In late fall 2011, Drake toured a handful of East Coast college campuses. Drake prefers playing smaller concerts. "I fought really hard for this tour because, of course [the record label] want[s] me to go get the big bucks, go into the stadiums and cash out," Drake told *MTV News* before hitting the road. "But I was just like, I really made this album for the same people that supported me since day one."

▲ Drake arrives at the 2009 GQ Men of the Year Awards. The following year, he would win one of the awards himself.

And the Winner Is...

While working on promoting his singing career, Drake has been racking up awards in his name. He has won BET awards for Best Male Hip-Hop Artist and Best Group (both in 2010), the latter for being a part of Young Money. At the BET Hip Hop Awards, Drake won Track of the Year for "Every Girl" (2009), as well as Rookie of the Year (2009) and MVP of the Year (2010). He won *GQ*'s Man of the Year in 2010. At the *Billboard* Music Awards, he won two awards in 2009, for both Top Rap Song and Top New Hip-Hop/ R & B Artist.

In 2011, he won eight awards, as Songwriter of the Year, and for multiple songs. The MuchMusic Video Awards is an annual award presented by the Canadian Music Channel, for the year's best music videos. Drake has won three awards and seven nominations, the most of any artist. In 2010, he won Record of the Year for "Unthinkable," at the Soul Train Music Awards. The Hal David Starlight Award, on behalf of the Songwriters Hall of Fame, is given yearly to talented songwriters. Drake won this award in 2011.

Back on the Road

Drake's *Club Paradise* tour kicked off on Valentine's Day 2012. He was joined by Kendrick Lamar and A$AP Rocky. Fans snapped up tickets. They couldn't wait to see their favorite singer live. Drake visited Europe in March and April. He toured through the spring. Then he did some U.S. gigs in May. Touring can be difficult, but Drake's family, friends and fans keep him strong.

▲ Drake accepts the award for Best Male Hip Hop Artist at the 2010 BET Awards.

Family, Friends, Fans, & Fame

Drake was very close to his maternal grandmother, Evelyn Sher. He mentions her in a few of his songs. When he signed his record deal, he couldn't wait to tell her. He rushed to visit his "Bubby" in a nursing home. (Bubby, which is often spelled differently than the way Drake spells it, means "Grandma" in Yiddish.) They talked about old times, like when they would do crossword puzzles together. Drake helped pay for her care. He told her now he could buy her anything she wanted. He's finally made it big. All Drake's grandma asked for was a hug and kiss.

Sadly, Drake's grandma died on Thanksgiving 2012. After she passed away, he tweeted, "Rest in peace to my grandmother Evelyn Sher. What a day to go. Thankful to have the times we did."

His grandma's voice appears on his song, "Look What You've Done." At the very end, a voicemail message can be heard. She thanks him for all he's done. "[I want] to let you know how grateful I am for your help in keeping me in this comfortable place. All I can say, Aubrey, is I remember the good times we had together. And the times I used to look after you. And I still have wonderful feelings about that. So God bless you, and I hope I'll see you."

The song is a tribute to his mom, grandma, and Uncle Steve. He thanks them for their love and support. He talks about how it was to see his mom so sick. Weakening bones that connect her spine and neck caused her to walk with a cane. He mentions getting her a much-needed operation. This was to help repair different bones and joints. He talks about how he finally took her to Rome.

Family First

Drake's mom has been ill for years. This worries Drake. They're super close. They've been through a lot together. He's the type of son who'll do anything for his mom. When Sandi had surgery, Drake canceled his 2010 European tour. He stayed with her while she recovered. He has said in interviews that her illness scares him. He hates seeing her in pain.

Family will always come first for Drake. When Backstreet Boys' Nick Carter lost his younger sister, Leslie, he said the show must go on. He missed her funeral. When Drake's mom needed surgery, he decided to reschedule his summer 2010 British and European tour dates. He announced this just one day before his performance at a big festival in Norway.

"Despite my best hopes, it is apparent that my mother will need surgery earlier than anticipated," Drake told the press. "In light of this news, I have made the difficult decision to cancel [the] tour in order to support her during her recovery, just as she supported me through the years. I cannot thank my European fans enough and look forward to performing abroad soon. I ask everyone to please respect my family's privacy during this time."

Drake Online

"Some of my favorite rappers, some of my heroes—DJ Screw, Aaliyah—there might be like 200 pictures of them because there was no Internet. Whereas with us, it's like every moment is documented," Drake told GQ magazine. Drake wonders if the Web sometimes makes it too easy for people to become famous.

The Internet has helped make many hopefuls famous. Justin Bieber, Greyson Chance, and Rebecca Black have YouTube to thank for their stardom. For Drake, it's MySpace. Drake can credit the social media Web site for helping him land a record deal.

▶ *Both Drake and Justin Bieber used sites like MySpace and YouTube to help them get famous.*

Drake's Twitter Marriage

Drake and record label mate, Nicki Minaj, really got fans talking in the summer of 2010. It started when Drake tweeted, "Please refer to @nickiminaj as Mrs. Aubrey Drake Graham and dont stare at her too long. She's finally mine. :)." Nicki admitted, "Yes, it's true. Drake and I tied the knot."

The loving tweets between Drake and Nicki became big news. Everyone was talking about it. Web sites like *Just Jarred* and *TMZ* were buzzing. Fans wondered about the tweets.

A day later, Nicki came clean. She joked, "My husband Drake and I have decided to have our marriage annulled." Their reps told the press the singers were just playing a prank on fans. The tweets got a lot of attention from

◄ *Drake's friend Nicki Minaj is a successful singer herself. Here, she performs in New York City's Time Square on April 6, 2012.*

the press. Later Drake told *Elle* magazine, "I don't know if we were really pretending. I'd marry Nicki. I think Nicki would be one of the only people that would understand me at the end of all of this and be able to love me."

On an episode of MTV2's *Sucker Free Countdown*, Drake mentioned always having a crush on Nicki. He added that she always saw him as a brother. Nicki later denied it on MTV2, saying, "Drake does not have a crush on me. Drake knows how to get you guys' attention."

Drake Talks Twitter & Tumblr

The Internet helped make Drake famous. But Drake isn't a big fan of social media sites. He thinks Twitter, Facebook, and Tumblr are an easy way to hurt others. Twitter allows people to post short messages publicly to followers. Drake uses Twitter to talk to his fans.

Celebrities use Twitter to keep their fans in the know. When Drake first began using Twitter, he was @Drakkardnoir. In September 2011, he dropped the name and changed to @Drake. He told fans, "Made the switch to @Drake ... feeling super official."

Drake doesn't like when people use Twitter to act mean. He thinks it's easy for people to hide behind their computer and be cruel. "...Like, you know you're going to see something bad. Out of 1,000 compliments, it's so crazy ... It's basically, like, when you used to sit there as a kid, and want to know what everyone is thinking. That's your superpower. [Twitter is] knowing what everyone is thinking." And sadly, sometimes those comments can really hurt people, even celebrities like Drake.

Find Him on Facebook

Drake also uses Facebook to talk to fans. He posts tour dates and shares his thoughts. When he heard Whitney Houston passed away, Drake's Facebook status read, "RIP Whitney." Facebook lets his fans comment on his posts, videos, or photos.

Drake is very sensitive. This also comes out in his songs. "When I was in my mom's house, I had nowhere to go, no real obligations," Drake told GQ. "My girlfriend at the time, if she was mad at me, my day was all [messed] up. I didn't have anything else. And that made for some of the best music, I think, to date. Records where I felt small."

The rapper is often made fun of for being emotional. For example there are two silly parody videos of Drake on YouTube. One shows a cartoon Drake angry and upset over Facebook comments. The other shows a Drake look-alike upset over the new Facebook layout. For most people, it's never a nice feeling being ridiculed, but Drake laughs it off and knows it comes with being famous.

Drake and His Fans

Drake has more than 25 million Facebook fans. Drake has the best fans. When he updates his Facebook status, fifty thousand fans click "Like" or leave a comment. They retweet his tweets.

They quote his lyrics. They make his albums go platinum. What is it people love about Drake? Some like his deep, sensitive lyrics. Some are drawn to his smooth vocals.

He's open to changing his style, but only if it makes his fans happy. "I had a bad habit of looking down at the ground when I performed, people started talking about it." To fix that, Drake began making eye contact with his fans. When he sings, he wants each audience member to feel special.

▼ *Drake signs copies of his album* Take Care *for his fans on November 14, 2011.*

Stars Love Drake

Celebrities love Drake. He's on their iPods. They tweet with him. Some even have crushes on the cute Canadian. MTV's *Jersey Shore* star Snooki does! In 2010, she told *OK* magazine he was her crush.

His *Ice Age 4* costar, Keke Palmer, told *Access Hollywood Live*, "I really wanted to meet Drake because he plays like, my little love interest. Isn't that so cool? I've always been a big fan of Drake since he was on *Degrassi*," Keke said.

Perhaps one of Drake's earliest known romantic interests was Keshia Chante, a fellow Canadian singer. He told *MuchMusic*, "Would I call Keshia Chante an ex? I'd be proud to say she is an ex. I am proud to say we had our time, when we were, like 16 years old. She's great. She's one of the first people in the industry that I met, we just connected."

Rihanna was linked to Drake for five months in 2009. Celebrity blogs said they were seen out and about together. However, during an interview with Angie Martinez, Rihanna said, "I definitely was attracted to Drake, but I think it is what it is—like it was what it was ... I just didn't want to get too serious with anything or anyone at that time."

Tennis star Serena Williams had a crush on the singer during his 2010 tour. Drake and Serena were seen playing tennis together. In November 2011 he told *Complex* that he "really, really loves and cares for her. She's definitely in my life and I'm in her life."

The end of 2011 brought a new relationship for Drake. He began dating model Dollicia Bryan. They met at her birthday party earlier in the year—he had stopped by since his DJ was spinning at the party.

Drake 💛 Nicki

Drake and Nicki Minaj have been close for a while. She sings with him on "Make Me Proud." Nicki has joined him onstage many times. They appeared on *Saturday Night Live* together. Nicki is very special to Drake. He admits she's perfect for him. What's more, his mom adores her. Nicki "gets" Drake.

He's called her his dream girl. Nicki insists they're just friends. Magazines say they've been seen cuddling. Some reports say they've even been spotted kissing. Could they one day date? Will they ever really get married? Only time will tell.

Famous Feuds

Drake doesn't hold back when he has an opinion. He's had several public feuds with other rappers. He's had issues with actor/rapper Common. He's had beef with Ludacris.

The problem with Common began when Common hinted about a certain soft rapper. Many rappers poke fun at other performers in their lyrics. Drake took offense. By February 2012, Common squashed the ongoing feud. "It's over. But it was all in the art of Hip Hop," Common told Fuse Network. "He said some things to me so I had to say some things back." He added, "I wouldn't say [he started it] but I know I heard something that I felt was

◄ Ludacris (pictured) and Drake battled over their difference through their song lyrics.

directed to me so I addressed it. That's all. But you know, thank God we were able to move forward from it and all is good."

It later came out that Serena Williams may have been behind the dispute. Common dated the tennis pro off and on for three years. He wasn't happy to hear she was hanging out with Drake.

Drake once mentioned that he felt rappers were starting to copy his style. Famous rapper Ludacris fought back with his song "Badaboom." He rapped, "Counterfeit rappers say I'm stealing their flows / But I can't steal what you never made up..." Ludacris suggested that this particular rapper hides behind Twitter. He dared the rapper to "say it to my face."

Drake replied to Ludacris's diss telling *Vibe* magazine, "[Ludacris,] that's a case of someone trying to use my marketing money to get things going again for themselves." He explained, "That didn't affect my day, my month, my year. I didn't take any of that seriously."

Though he's had some drama with artists, he also has a long list of friends in the biz. He's worked with other singers and recording artists. He has written and collaborated with Alicia Keys, Jamie Foxx, Dr. Dre, Mario Winans, Kanye West, Eminem, and Jay-Z.

Crazy Fame

In 2010, Drake grabbed some tea at a mall in St. Louis. Fans saw him and started following him. The group grew so large, mall security asked Drake to leave. "I feel like maybe two months ago, I still had a bit of anonymity. Now it's a hassle to do regular things," Drake told Macleans.ca. "I don't know if it will ever feel normal. But I've accepted my responsibility—it's what I wanted, it's what I dreamed about."

This is typical. A near riot happened when Drake was spotted at a Minneapolis mall in December 2011. Word got out that Drake and Lil Wayne were there. News Web sites say two hundred shoppers went wild at the Mall of America. Tables and chairs were thrown. People were hurt and ten arrests were made.

Wherever Drake goes, fans will follow. On the New Year's Eve that rang in 2012, a big crowd formed at Dream Downtown hotel. The *New York Daily News* reported it took ten security guards to safely move Drake from one place to another.

Giving Back & Future Focused

Drake doesn't mind using his fame to help others. He's always looking for ways to give back. He visits sick kids in the hospital. He performs at fund-raisers. He makes generous donations to charities and more.

SPEAK UP!

Even before he was a big rap star, Drake was doing good deeds. After his *Degrassi* character was shot by a fellow student, Drake began working with SPEAK UP. SPEAK UP is an anonymous hotline created by The Center to Prevent Youth Violence. SPEAK UP works to prevent youth violence in schools and communities.

Drake appeared in special TV ads aimed at teens. These commercials warned young people about the dangers of weapons in school. He said, "In 75% of school shootings, the attacker told someone what they were gonna do."

Drake tells young viewers to please tell someone. Tell a teacher. Tell a counselor. To remain anonymous, call 1-866-SPEAKUP. Since 2002, SPEAK UP has gotten more than 38,000 calls from kids nationwide.

Young Artists for Haiti

On January 12, 2010, an earthquake shook Haiti. The deadly quake affected 3 million people, killing 316,000, injuring 300,000, and leaving one million homeless. Everyone from everywhere wanted to help. From concerts to fund-raiser telethons, celebrities raised money for survivors.

◀ *Drake in Toronto, Canada, on November 14, 2011.*

Young Artists for Haiti was a group of young Canadian musicians. They all shared one goal. They hoped to help raise awareness for Haiti relief. In February, more than fifty Canadian singers and musicians gathered at The Warehouse Studio in Vancouver, British Columbia. The group, including Justin Bieber and Avril Lavigne, recorded a unique version of K'naan's "Wavin' Flag."

Drake was a very important part of Young Artists for Haiti. His rapping lyrics added a sweet touch to the super group's song. "This project means something to me," Drake told reporters. "It's Canadian ... It's a great song ... as an incredible song, an incredible piece of music will generate interest and hopefully we can raise money and help."

"Wavin' Flag" debuted at number one on the Canadian Hot 100. It is the third song in the chart's history to debut at number one. This song helped Drake and the Canadian musicians raise more than one million dollars for Canadian charities. Funds raised went toward helping Haiti.

SickKids Ambassador

In December 2010, Drake spread holiday cheer at Toronto's Hospital for Sick Children. The young patients got to meet the singer. He signed autographs and posed for photos. Drake believes that music can help heal the sick. He spoke to the children about a special Music Therapy program at SickKids. The program helps them cope during difficult times.

Drake is an ambassador to the SickKids Music Therapy program. He raised $70,000 for the SickKids Friends of Music Therapy Endowment Fund. A portion of ticket sales from his *Light Dreams and Nightmares* tour was donated to the cause.

Drake Helps President Clinton

Back in March 2011, Drake teamed up with President Bill Clinton for a special event. The singer performed for the Clinton Foundation's Millennium Network. The fund-raiser featured a variety of celebs. It was held at Hollywood's Boulevard3 on Sunset Boulevard. Jamie Foxx, Maroon 5's Adam Levine, Bradley Cooper, and Kristen Bell also attended.

The Clinton Foundation inspires students to work toward change. Funds raised during the course of the event benefit the Millennium Network. This foundation urges students and activists under 45 to get involved. The organization focuses on problems like climate change and childhood obesity. President Clinton welcomed guests and started the evening off. Drake ended it with a performance.

Drake and Lil Wayne perform at the 2011 BET Awards. ▶

41

Drake Gives Back to Toronto

A proud Canadian, Drake has a soft spot for his hometown, Toronto. In the summer of 2011, Drake was the winner of Toronto's Allan Slaight Award for achievement by a young Canadian. The award comes with $10,000. Drake donated the prize money to Dixon Hall. Dixon Hall helps folks in low-income areas of Toronto. Drake told Toronto.com, "I am a proud Canadian, and I am grateful to Canada's Walk of Fame and the Slaight Foundation for this award."

Holiday Giving

On December 17, 2011, Drake joined music legend Stevie Wonder at his House Full of Toys charity event. Drake and Wonder already had a bit of history. Wonder plays harmonica on "Doing It Wrong" on Drake's *Take Care* album. "Stevie Wonder even talking to me at first was obviously one of the most surreal things in the world," Drake told *Rolling Stone*. "Then being willing to make music with me, it's very, very flattering, very surreal. And he's such a great guy," he added.

At the charity, Drake introduced Wonder saying, "Ladies and gentlemen, please make some noise for the man of the hour, the man of the year, the man of the century, in my opinion, one of the greatest musicians of all time, Stevie Wonder."

Drake must have been filled with holiday joy in December 2011. He also donated $25,000 toward building a learning center in Jamaica. Drake shot the video for his hit song "Find Your Love" in Kingston, Jamaica, with dancehall artist, Mavado.

Drake told *The Jamaica Star* he "just wanted to show back some love by helping out with Mavado's project on the Gullyside." The singer added, "It's a very positive move and something I am very happy to be a part of. Education is the key to life so to be able to assist in that process is very fulfilling." The learning center will be named after Drake and Mavado. It will include a computer lab and library.

Drake's Special Visit

While touring America, Drake made a surprise visit to a Nashville high school. He wanted to inspire students. On February 17, 2012, Drake visited Martin Luther King Magnet High School and encouraged the students to stay in school. The kids were happy and shocked to see a big star at their school.

"My inspiration in life is my family and my friends," Drake told the students. They yelled and cheered. "If I could do

Drake speaks at the 54th ▶ *Annual Grammy Awards in 2012.*

two things in my life that I have never done, one is learn how to play the piano. And two, I put this on my life, be able to bring my mother a high school diploma." Having a mom who was a teacher made it hard for Drake to feel good about his choice to drop out of school.

During his visit, Drake wowed students with a special gift. He had ten tickets to his Nashville concert. This made the kids cheer so loudly. Before the singer said good-bye, he had one last tip for the kids. He told them to always follow their dreams. "You never know what could happen," the star said.

Future Plans

Drake doesn't take his success for granted. Growing up, he would watch MTV and think the money, fans, and touring were magical. "That's who's sitting on that album cover, that kid that's just somehow gone from his mom's basement in Toronto to becoming a king," Drake told *GQ* magazine in disbelief.

Drake wants to do it all. He wants to be more than just a famous rapper. "I care about acting a lot so I'm excited to get back into it," Drake told *XXL Magazine*. In the summer of 2012, he voiced the part of Ethan in the animated kid's film *Ice Age 4: Continental Drift*. If a movie was ever made about President Barack Obama, Drake would love to play him. Some of his fans may be surprised to know that Drake also sees himself in funny movies. "I love comedy and comedic timing," Drake told 94.9's

Drake watches the Dallas Mavericks take on the Sacramento Kings on March 9, 2012. ▶

WiLD JAM. "I just want to do a good comedy film, whether it's a Judd Apatow [or] dry humor film. I'm definitely shaking the right hands and meeting the right people."

In addition to acting, Drake has said he wouldn't mind being a professional chef one day. He's also said he can see himself owning a Toronto restaurant or hotel. But whatever he does, Drake wants to stick around. "My biggest priority is longevity … That is the key." Drake told the *Toronto Sun*.

Drake doesn't want to be popular for only a short time. He wants fans to love him for years to come. "There are people who had success and let it go. The success I've achieved thus far is great. But I know people could forget about it all tomorrow. They can forget they ever loved Drake. I can't let that happen. I won't let that happen," he added.

Speaking of success, Drake was nominated in three categories at the 55th Annual Grammy Awards. They included Best Rap Performance, Best Rap Song and Best Rap Album,

As far as music is concerned, his fans don't have to worry. According to Drake, "I'm motivated by success. I'm still growing and learning and my vulnerability in my music is the key to keeping me humble, grounded, and proud to be here."

Further Info

Books

Earl, C. F. *Drake*. Philadelphia, PA: Mason Crest, 2012.

Kennedy, Robert. *Drake*. New York: Gareth Stevens Pub., 2012.

Peppas, Lynn. *Drake*. New York: Crabtree, 2012.

Internet Addresses

DizzyDrake.org
   <www.drizzydrake.org>

Drake's Offical Web Site
   <www.drakeofficial.com>

Connect With Drake
   Official Twitter: <twitter.com/DRAKE>
   Official Facebook: <facebook.com/Drake>

Index